Superstars
of the
ATLANTA
BRAVES

by Max Hammer

amicus
high interest

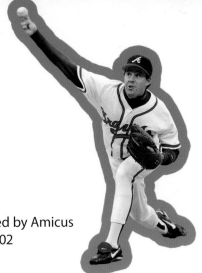

Amicus High Interest is published by Amicus
P.O. Box 1329, Mankato, MN 56002
www.amicuspublishing.us

Library of Congress Cataloging-in-Publication Data
Hammer, Max.
  Superstars of the Atlanta Braves / by Max Hammer.
      pages cm. -- (Pro sports superstars)
  Includes index.
  Summary: "Presents some of the Atlanta Braves' greatest players and
their achievements in pro baseball, including Chipper Jones, Andruw
Jones, and Jason Heyward"--Provided by publisher.
  ISBN 978-1-60753-590-4 (hardcover) -- ISBN 978-1-60753-624-6 (pdf
ebook)
  1. Atlanta Braves (Baseball team)--History--Juvenile literature. I. Title.
  GV875.A8H35 2014
  796.357'6409758231--dc23
                          2013044097

Photo Credits: Nick Wass/AP Images, cover; Tannen Maury/AP Images,
2, 14; Todd Kirkland/Icon SMI, 5; Bettmann/Corbis, 7; AP Images, 9; John
Bazemore/AP Images, 10, 22; John Swart/AP Images, 13; Dennis Poroy/AP
Images, 16; Tony Dejak/AP Images, 18; David Goldman/AP Images, 20

Produced for Amicus by The Peterson Publishing Company
and Red Line Editorial.

Editor Arnold Ringstad
Designer Maggie Villaume
Printed in the United States of America
Mankato, MN
2-2014
PA10001
10 9 8 7 6 5 4 3 2 1

TABLE OF CONTENTS

MEET THE ATLANTA BRAVES

The Atlanta Braves have been around for more than 100 years. The team has played in Atlanta since 1966. Many stars have played for the Atlanta Braves. Here are some of the best.

EDDIE MATHEWS

Eddie Mathews played third base. He was also a strong batter. He hit more than 30 **home runs** in nine straight seasons.

Mathews retired in 1968. He later became a Braves coach.

8

HENRY "HANK" AARON

Henry "Hank" Aaron hit 755 home runs. That was a record. Babe Ruth held the record before him. Aaron broke Ruth's record in 1974.

Aaron's nickname was "Hammerin' Hank."

TOM GLAVINE

Tom Glavine was a great pitcher. He won the **Cy Young Award** twice. It is given to the best pitchers. Glavine won it in 1991 and 1998.

Glavine was the MVP of the 1995 World Series. The Braves won.

JOHN SMOLTZ

John Smoltz could do it all. He won the Cy Young Award in 1996. He was a starting pitcher then. Later Smoltz became a great **closer**.

Smoltz had more than 200 wins and 150 saves. No other player has done both.

13

GREG MADDUX

Pitcher Greg Maddux had great control. He won three Cy Young Awards with the Braves. Maddux helped the Braves win the 1995 World Series.

Maddux won 18 Gold Glove Awards.

16

CHIPPER JONES

Chipper Jones played for 19 seasons. All were with the Braves. He played third base. His best season was in 1999. Jones won an MVP award that year.

Jones's real name is Larry. He got his nickname as a kid.

ANDRUW JONES

Andruw Jones played center field. He made diving catches. He was also a great hitter. Jones had 51 home runs in 2005.

JASON HEYWARD

Jason Heyward plays right field. He joined the Braves in 2010. He quickly became a star. He helped them reach the playoffs.

The Braves have had many great superstars. Who will be next?

TEAM FAST FACTS

Founded: 1876

Other names: Boston Red Stockings (1876–1882), Boston Beaneaters (1883–1906), Boston Doves (1907–1910), Boston Rustlers (1911), Boston Braves (1912–1935, 1941–1952), Boston Bees (1936–1940), Milwaukee Braves (1953–1965)

Home Stadium: Turner Field (Atlanta, Georgia)

World Series Championships: 3 (1914, 1957, and 1995)

Hall of Fame Players:
46, including
Eddie Mathews, Hank Aaron,
Greg Maddux, and Tom Glavine
(also 10 managers)

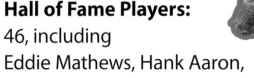

WORDS TO KNOW

closer – a player whose main job is to pitch at the end of the game to protect a lead

Cy Young Award – an award given to the best pitcher in each league after each season

Gold Glove Awards – awards given to the best fielders each year

home run – a hit that goes far enough to leave the field, letting the hitter run all the way around the bases to score a run

MVP – Most Valuable Player; an honor given to the best player each season

saves – games won by pitchers who hold a lead at the end of a game

World Series – the annual baseball championship series

LEARN MORE

Books

Gilbert, Sara. *World Series Champs: Atlanta Braves*. Mankato, MN: Creative Education, 2013.

Kelley, K. C. *Atlanta Braves (Favorite Baseball Teams)*. North Mankato, MN: The Child's World, 2014.

Web Sites

Atlanta Braves—Official Site
http://atlanta.braves.mlb.com
Watch video clips and read stories about the Atlanta Braves.

Baseball History
http://mlb.mlb.com/mlb/history/
Learn more about the history of baseball.

MLB.com
http://mlb.com
See pictures and track your favorite baseball player's stats.

INDEX